THE KILIM
DREAMING

THE KILIM
DREAMING

ROBERT HILL LONG

THE DOROTHY BRUNSMAN POETRY PRIZE
BEAR STAR PRESS

Inquiries may be directed to

BEAR STAR PRESS
185 Hollow Oak Drive
Cohasset, CA 95973
www.bearstarpress.com

Cover art: Kilim image courtesy of the collection of
Dr. Ayan and Brigitte Gülgönen, Istanbul

Book design: Beth Spencer

Author photograph: Ranee Ruble

The publisher would like to acknowledge Dorothy Brunsman
for her support of the press since its inception.

ISBN: 978-0-9793745-6-2
Library of Congress Control Number: 2010924135

To my whippoorwill
thirty years west of Carolina Beach

CONTENTS

THE SPEAR LILY

She may not be arranged. Wooed, seduced, fêted, yes—
but taken home always afterward. One may phone
the following morning, one may send oranges;
she prefers cut flowers. Prefers to sleep alone,
the longest standing arrangement she trusts. She stays
outside herself enough to see that the concoction
of glamour-makeup stills she flipped through in those
waiting rooms, appointed for the correction
of her teeth and eyes and spine, have recomposed her
as a thing. The girl slouch, crossed incisors and eyes
have been straightened into this object that takes care
in being seen and self-attended in cafés.
She takes two coffees. Between them, the clean white mold
of the ashtray. She does not smoke. One coffee grows cold.

The second coffee is a signal that her night is free.
When she is booked, she orders only one to go.
Her list of clients is kept up by the maître-d'
and certain gallery owners. When she takes two
plastic flutes of wine at an opening, they phone
around their copy of the list until they find
a yes to her discreet standing invitation,
for a small percentage. This arrangement takes her mind
off secretarial chores. She can concentrate
on paintings, having dresses made. Her galleries
favor figurative works—women at toilet,
reclining nudes, seated couples whose lowered eyes
ignore the table strewn with appetites or leavings.
The dressmaker cuts her lines like an engraving.

The yes-man sends a cab to the gallery
or café. The one surprise she lets him sustain
is where he'll take her: he'll have her in the taxi
on the bridge to Sausalito, stop for champagne,
then resume the entertainments on the long drive
around the Bay. Wine growers know her from tastings,
Puerto Rican coffee merchants treat her to live
sex shows with dogs and Filipino girls wasting
their cries on solo men with raincoats in their laps.
Her cost ensures grace and wit in weird positions.
She knows how to make *Yes* and *No* sound like *Perhaps*.
Her yoga teacher showed her how all propositions
solve themselves in practice: Hold the breath and heartbeat
back, then the rest relaxes into willing meat.

Today she's at the arboretum. In one garden
a spear lily rears its red spike twelve feet above
her practiced footfalls. She almost feels it harden
inside her like a second go at making love
with one of those safe strangers who let her go home
to sleep off his grateful face. But she cannot
evade the question it poses to her—this crime
against nature, shaped not so much to penetrate
her sex as to split her in half from sole to skull,
to spit her on its tusk and spill her catalogue
of meat and makeup, cocktail fucks and sleeping pills.
She stands transfixed and flimsy as a slip of fog
speared by the TransAmerica spire. The lily's force
is asking: *When you wake, who knows which face is yours?*

How many faces had she tried on while waiting
for this or that specialist to reconstruct her
crooked original to a mask inviting
lavish men to pay for long nights dissecting her
enigma? *Cosmo, Vogue, Elle*—she is built of parts
scavenged from the graveyard of glossy eight-by-tens
in the surgeon's office lounge. All of the hearts
she has let beat heavily against her pretense
fly home to kids and wives, convention weekends done,
expense accounts doctored. Unnamed but itemized,
she's left like a men's magazine on the airplane:
it will get picked up again. No one reads it twice.
That is not what she thought beneath the spear lily.
She flashed on this: *I bought a face. I have no country.*

Her arboretum escort is Dutch, balding, gay,
sentenced to wholesale Javanese spice and coffees
in California. He was scared of HIV
and homesick. This garden, these foggy colonies
of South Pacific exotica, were meant to bring
this companionable woman home to the mother
he'd buried beneath monkey-puzzle trees last spring.
He guessed she'd like the break from sex, from the summer
city's glare, the streets and freeway interchanges
smog-jammed, a pretzel-bag burst by all the traffic—
tourists, shore-leave sailors, huge trucks stuffed with oranges.
He was kind, celibate, unprepared for the panic
paralyzing her. How could this great peaceable
bloom that cures his exile bring her face such trouble?

It was her city, but no longer her land: these green
labia tonguing the fog-colored air she knew
less well with each breath. This sexless man's garden
was Indonesia, New Zealand, Chile, cool strange stew
of ages, great bristly cycads and horsetails huge
as sloths and mammoths. She felt an urge to run straight
to the chiropractor, to grab her cell phone and page
the oral surgeon who reclined her with his foot
pedal's soundless calm, and built the glassblower O
of her perfect mouth. She wants to reconfine
her rendezvous to the café, to the art show,
no, limit herself to the one stem of wine
and simply leaf through the catalogue of old prints
and provenances. The Dutch man's smile is no defense.

"What is it?" he asks. "I'm sorry, I don't know how
this hurts you—you're hurting, aren't you? Maybe we
should walk to the Japanese pagoda now,
there is a teahouse. The tea ceremony
was made for this. I am prepared to supervise—,"
he hunts for a less clinical phrase, more soothing,
"I wish to help." Extends his hand. "Tea calms twice:
as you make it, first, as your hand does the whisking
of fine powders through the water; then as you empty
the bowl through the bamboo filter and feel your mind
clear in the cup. Then you drink in peace. Oh, that's three
ways tea works, yes? Come," he smiles, "let me be kind.
There is no threat in tea leaves." She makes herself shake
her head. Then whispers, "Please. Let me return your check."

He shakes his head in return, raises both palms
like a Buddha: a manicured gesture that forbids
even as it greets, to silence what overwhelms
speech but not the desire to speak. His eyelids,
she notices, have closed—like a john riding
his pleasure-wave to its break-point, she thinks, and starts
to laugh at the ridiculous image she's hiding—
and he says: "No peace in the world, until our hearts
find they are broken by the world. I paid you for
an afternoon outside myself. Now you give me
something more. Loss, I think. You let me see your fear."
He opens his eyes to hers. "The whole mystery
and glamour your work makes you project, the expert spell—
it falls away, yes? Show me where you are in hell."

She holds one palm to her head. The other she points flat
toward its surroundings—the astringencies
of eucalyptus, the spiky bromeliads,
odorless explosions of green and cerise:
hell is both too easy and too old a word
to convey this breathlessness, this stun, arresting
face and voice and limbs. The garden has interred
her body in a moment foreign to the years nesting
her agreement with silence about the life.
Silence superseded the sex work, the replies—
choreographed, athletic, like a dream-wife—
she was expected to proffer. Silence was the vise
that clamped her safety shut. Silence ends in hell
here. Hell is not men. Then what does she have to tell?

She told the men: *Treat me like your exorcist.*
The rich means you invest me with to make you come
bring death. When you die between my legs, all you missed
floods through me, an afterbirth of blood and slime
equal to each dollar you misspent in this waste
of lust—she has read Shakespeare's sex-terror sonnet—
that turns like bad milk into a woe you will taste
each time you nail your mouth to your wife's sour clit.
You will see your tongue winging my spirit-dove
and feel my thighs close on your ears, and never hear
your children cry out in their beds they need your love
to save them from the tall shade who sucks their bones clear
from their skins. She said this with arms and looks and breath.
The lily repeats it back, her sentence of death.

She has not spoken this aloud, yet the Dutch man
keeps nodding as though he has gone inside her
thought, as though he knows where this crisis began,
how long since. Now she sees why. "You were a hooker?"
she asks, and knows his answer. "Where was it, when
did you quit—no, that's not the question: Did you quit?
And can you please quit nodding?" How could he divine
what she can't bring herself to say unless he knew it
with his mouth and hands, unless her stratagems
once were his as well? "I don't want tea," she says. "I want
to know how your story fits mine." The dry limbs
of the eucalyptus clatter. "What if I can't—,"
he pauses, "tell you any secret you don't know?"
"Pretend it's strip poker," she says. "I call. You show."

~ 2 ~

Begin in a restaurant in Amsterdam.
A pretty boy who busses tables and assists
at early Mass. A priest who loves his leg of lamb
with mint paste. One morning after the boy has kissed
the Communion implements, the priest asks for help
with his robe. Naked we came into the world,
he says, and naked we leave. I see how you gulp
the leftover wine. In a moment they lie curled
on the rug, the priest drinking from the boy's fountain.
The priest has an allowance from his Flemish father,
he pays handsomely for this silent chore again
and again. He teaches one trick, then another.
They are seen touching one night at the restaurant.
The priest is transferred. The boy's transformed into a cunt.

His complaisant talent turns to practiced skill
at spotting lonely marks at dinner. He grazes
their shoulders, pouring their water. Masters the drill
of negotiating an hour's value. Glazes
over at well-timed instants, goes limp or grows hard
as the occasion demands. Learns how to dress well.
Increases profits, recruiting from the schoolyard—
younger, prettier faces. He rings a bell
like a priest himself and willing boys share a piece
of themselves for a smaller piece of what plays.
In eight years he drives a Saab, keeps a good address.
Sets his own hours. Discovers the word *No.* Says
Yes expensively. He's twenty-three. He goes to Mass
to show off what came of letting Christ kiss his ass.

A bishop wears a frock for him. An archbishop
begs for silk handcuffs and strict correction. His plan,
he tells his B-boy crew, is to trick his way up
the College of red-robes into the Vatican,
then get a book and made-for-TV-movie deal
and retire: Mallorca, Saint Maartens, Hollywood.
The boys laugh. Then the youngest lies in hospital
and smiles at their party stories under a hood
full of oxygen. Before he dies, another
is confined to his last bed on the same ward.
He finds himself taking up quilting, like a mother
whose sons turn casualties, their enemy a crossword
verb whose clue is *Gives comfort.* The verb becomes noun,
the noun all parts of speech: waters where his boys drown.

His sentence: to remain untouched. And celibate.
And watch his disco-boys fuck their oblivion,
eyes wide, until the hospice drugs terminate
all distinctions between their dreams of going one
step further than he, and dying while they take God
doggie-style before the saints and archangels.
For all he knows, they do. The ritual clod
of clay drops from his hands, these untouchables
he vows in private to deprive forever
bringing any boy's mannish appetite beneath
his killing care. He meets an old client, after
buying what he wishes were his last graveyard wreath,
a Java coffee planter home for sport. "I think
you can be salvaged," the man says. "Buy me a drink."

All he set aside for his island future gets
converted into coffee futures, and a title:
junior partner and chief purveyor for the West
Coast, the chance to purge mistakes in true colonial
fashion in the country of second chances.
Home he remakes in a carriage house behind
the planter's ocean-hillside mansion. Advances
on his American salary pay for his half-blind
mother to sail with her Hummel figurines
and antimacassars to the last port she will
ever see—intense Pacific blues and greens
merging with her diabetic mists until
her breath is pacified to smoke. He plants her ash,
flies east. His coffee-jet, a coffin crammed with cash.

Cash in metric tons of Java, Arabica,
Ethiopia, Kenya, Jamaica Blue Mountain,
Costa Rica, Guatemala, Colombia—
the old failsafe—he controls a black fountain
of acids and bitterness, fruit of the Third World
stripped to its seed, roasted in little hell-ovens
and sealed in blister-bags, hundreds of tiny turds
per kilo, each split down its backside like mens'
beautiful dark identical buttocks. Each bean
concentrates the oldest odor of sweat—
sweat of work, of sex—all there has ever been,
that wanted to take America on: the bet
he sees embodied in coffee-colored faces
here, like him, to bury their immigrant traces.

Diego, Mahmoud, Puraya, Jahmon: he hears
their names ground down to the American grit
of Dick and Mack and Phil and Jack, names of queers
common as new pennies dropped in the gutter. They hit
the concrete with a clink, spin a few bright turns
and lie face up like Lincoln, shot in the theater.
In the back of their blown-open heads are urns
filled with the ash of Asia and Africa
and Central America, a memorial
to expectations great as marble or granite.
They smog the city like inexhaustible
soot of bus and taxi and van. They're the shit
and scrap and trash the massive white curb sweepers splash
through iron storm grates back into the Bay's brown wash.

"We," he tells her, "who are foreign by birth, and strangers
by nature—we're infiltrators. We need cities
to steep our homeless passions. We lie in mangers
of gospel missions until some wise man pities
our child-of-god features with frankincense and myrrh
and gold. Gold is the main dream of our sleeping meat,
isn't it? but what dreamer doesn't want a hit of pure
perfume as well? To have beauty complete
the sum of desire and furnish this homeless house,
this queer unnatural meat, with reason enough
to crawl out of its poor bunk the next day and rouse
a trick or two to buy breakfast. The trade is rough
and breaks most of us in half faster than the years
cash in our looks, and leave our poor pasts in arrears.

"Self-doubt is the biggest debt we have to work out,
but when you trade the birth-gift of identity
to trick an American fortune, you come out
as a pretense still, a demographic entity
the city uses to make a name for itself,
and a moral statistic the church wants to kill
with hellfire. Or sexless charity. You're the waif
they mean to save with a wafer—that bread pill,
that tasteless, half-baked god designed to transfuse
your poison blood with a shot of communion wine,
plus ARVs if you can't afford to refuse
the one serum without the others. We do fine—
you and I—we're the fraction who solved the problem
alone. The rest get screwed. And we help deny them.

"My mother was a whore, too. Only once. The john
was a Calvinist preacher with a wife and three
legitimate heirs. If he claimed me as his son
he'd have to deny his church and his family—
surrender his preordained pension, plus the keys
to his townhouse, English sedan, gentlemen's club,
not to mention the one Saint Peter lent him. Please—,"
he pats her hand, "I'm almost done. I had to scrub
my heart inside out. Otherwise you'd believe me
just a sympathizer with nothing more to prove
than a passing ability to show pity
for a whore. Pity, my mother taught me, is one remove
from love. A hateful remove, she said, worse than hate.
Pity your father, and hate me. But love the fate

that lets you keep my name and love, and forces you
to build character out of the ruins of this
divine joke. Your father is more bastard than you.
But without him you would lack a mother to kiss
good night, and know you are blessed by her, at least."
He is quiet at last. The sun has been out awhile
now, she notices: the summer fog is erased,
the spear lily's shadow pointing like a sundial
to the city, her safe café and gallery,
as though signaling it's time, or past time for her
to choose the next move. Back there is the bed where she
can let this afternoon regress into nightmare,
then solve it with pills and tailored sheaths and dyed hair.
There's backward, and there's forward. And forward is where?

"I wish I had a car," she says. "A car that could think,
one of those future-intelligence fantasy
things that reads your thoughts and pulls you back from the brink
of your dumbest intuition and declares, 'See,
stepping on the gas here will get you nothing but
a final slow-motion plunge into the Pacific—
I'll just touch the brakes, and correct us to the right.'"
A machine to second-guess each impulse to flick
the wheel to cut a steep coast curve enough to make
her choice look like an accident. A machine to keep
her straight, in the right lane, without the chance to fake
oblivion as a driving error. The shape
her self-preserving takes: a box of glass and steel
will, to override her wish for suicide skill.

Nothing holds her here but the slightest pressure
of her companion's hand. She feels him letting go—
the air starts pressing her to the grass, to strain her
through its blades—, she wants to be felled, to slip below
thought like a nurse-log: succulents rooting her skin,
fattening their squat umbrellas; letting rain river
her spine and thigh bones to a minor canyon
of lime and gristle. . . . "Look," he says, "let's go before
I turn into an exotic topiary.
Not a bad fate maybe, but why ruin these new
Italian loafers?" She stares at his shoes. "Sorry,"
she manages. "Sorry I broke down here. Will you
let me take your arm?" A professional gesture:
but it lets her breathe the air that would have smashed her.

 3

Minutes later they are drinking a bowl of tea,
a green-gray powder he measured from a pouch
in his breast pocket. "Mama's ashes," he jokes. "Really,
it's green Ceylon mixed with poppy. Good for the couch
of lucid dreams you tell your shrink of the hour—
that's me. Except my hourly rate is zero,
nothing but the hour itself." She feels a flower
unfurl its paper of red petals in her slow
liquid brain, a drowse of calm, of clear picturings.
There is a girl at a small table in the grass,
writing. Spice of pears and bay laurel. A bird sings
Peter peter peter. The girl has left her class
napping in a white school in the burnt yellow hills
to practice writing a name. It's not her name she spells.

It is the name she wants to have when she is done
being a child. A girl with dirty feet and buck-teeth
whose good skirt gets washed each night. She has just one
of each thing her schoolmates own in multiples. The math
is simple, it subtracts her from their herd of smiles
and new clothes, the brisk trade in notes and sack lunches
and who gets invited over when the last bells
stop mocking her like good-girl voices, like bunches
of curls and ribbons swallowed by a station wagon.
One pair of shoes and a dusty road; one Bible—
not even a cookbook; one mother who stays gone
days at a time; one thin blanket, incapable
of cocooning her against her granddad's drunken paws,
or her mother's men, teaching her their midnight laws.

"Listen," she tells him, "I still know my Bible. Book
of Job, twenty-one, verses eleven through thirteen."
He nods. "*They send forth their little ones like a flock,
and their children dance. To the timbrel and harp they sing
and rejoice at the sound of the pipe. They spend their days
in prosperity, and in a moment they go
down to Sheol.* In my back row seat I'd send those
lucky station wagon kids straight to hell, with no
good mother to save them from dirty mouths and nails
scratching their panties down their skinny white shins.
In my daydream it was them who had the shovels
full of spunk like coals in their cunts, loaded in
each night. They were nailed spread-eagle, like me, by sex
until their ribbons and curls melted off like wax.

"Then I got caught putting all that into pictures.
We were supposed to be doing long division.
The teacher slipped behind me and saw the factors
I was using were big dicks and explosions
of little girl bodies. Off to the principal!
She yanked me down the hall by my ear, sat me hard
in the punishment chair. They threatened to call
my mother. What a laugh. They sent me to the yard
with my table and math book. I had to work there
while the principal drove to the police station.
The lunch lady took me home. She washed my hair
and let me sleep in her bed. 'Part of my mission,'
she said. 'Just call me Auntie.' My mother I saw
next at the hearing where she gave me up to the law.

"After that, it was three foster houses before
I landed a pair of grownups I liked as well
as they liked me. But in one I was a whore
in the woman's eyes and the man's hands, the old hell
all over again, in a nicer neighborhood.
In the next, there was an older foster brother
who claimed my karma would improve, giving head—
that I had to work through the bad taste of other
lives, worse than this one, in servicing the real needs
of boys like him, sucking the demon out of them.
A girl takes the devil inside, and then it bleeds
out of her and purifies him at the same time.
So he said. But I got assigned a new caseworker
who wasn't blind. She fixed up my last transfer."

The house was in the Berkeley flats, a female
anthropologist tenured in women's studies.
The caseworker led her ward through an entry hall
hung with goddess masks. "We're going to be buddies!"
a voice pealed from the living room, and she was swept
off her feet by a batik muumuu topped with black curls
and a laugh big as a welcome wagon. "I kept
the chicken roasting low until you got here, girls.
Are you hungry?" She was starved. She loaded her dish
with breasts and peas and thin-cut potatoes in schmaltz.
"I'm Carol," the woman said. "I swim like a flatfish,
work past midnight, and I love the Blue Danube Waltz—,"
the girl spritzed Sprite through her nose; "now, three secrets from you."
"Okay. Awful karma; the worst cramps; and I hate to screw."

This made the caseworker spritz water. "I rarely,"
she laughed, "hear the unspeakable stuff tumble forth
so soon in a home interview. You two barely
know each other, and already you've made this night worth
the trouble it took to make this match. I can sleep
better now, God knows I need it." She said goodnight.
Carol led the girl upstairs. On the bed, a heap
of chocolate kisses, teen magazines, a flashlight.
"I want you to get used to using your new bed
for reading at all hours. Bedtime has been your bane,
I hear. Now you can take a good book there instead
of a man. Around here there's a shortage of men,
though you'll meet my husband during the holidays.
We'll never divorce, and he'll never leave Santa Cruz."

≈ 4 ≈

"To marriages of convenience—," the Dutch man lifts
the last of his tea in a toast, "made in friendship
and compassion." Early evening. The small bright rafts
of tour groups and families float off in a last sip
of opiated tea. "And if I were to ask,
would you do that for me?" She studies his green eyes
for the hint of mockery cushioning the risk
in such a request. There is none. And no kind lies
lie between them, just a table in the last light,
two empty cups, a bowl of old nightmares reduced
to dregs, poppy ash, wet jade leaves in which the right
reply to their futures might still be found. Or lost.
"I believe," she says, "I'd have to give you a No
and sleep on the real Maybe until tomorrow."

She starts to rise. Automatic, filial, he stands first.
"Tomorrow, then. Are you famished? I hear the tree
of life got cloned and transplanted here. Even the worst
day improves with a good fruit salad. And a pie,
sliced warm from the New World's old dream-apple. I know
a place that does both close to perfection."
She nods. Evening sweeps them through the gate, two slow
wondering steps not quite in synch, their direction
the night outside paradise among the other
lost childhoods trying to make a path with crumbs and stones.
"You want to hear what happened to my stepmother,"
she says. "Yes," he answers, "tomorrow." The black bones
of Monterey pines close ranks behind them. And the spear
lily, faint torch in no angel's fist, smolders there.

THE BOOK OF JOEL

Parable of Luck

The beach house, when we drove up, was hedged with figs;
when we returned from our first swim, starlings clung
like predatory fruit to the fig bushes they'd stripped.

Then they exploded overhead in a ruckus
of wings and spiteful noise—nearly Biblical,
I thought, a parable of how sudden bad luck is.

And while we were swimming our young friend Joel
died. He was dancing in a club, he was eighteen,
his heart failed. His parents are religious people,

they know how, in the Book of Matthew, the fig tree
falls under this heading: *All these are the beginning
of sorrow.* It puts forth shoots, it is withered. *Weep,*

says the Book of Joel*, and the Lord will bring rain
and new wine.* Too brief a book. But God took Joel dancing.

I Try Not to Think About That

His green Goodwill tee read, *I May Not Be Perfect
But Parts of Me Are Excellent.* In his highchair
he directed breakfast-food plays: Joel's Toast Theater,
they named it. Like a benign Old Testament prophet

he called his big-eyed Fisher-Price figures "My people."
They left Texas at night, heading to Oregon:
"Sometimes it all seems like a dream," he said. "You mean
driving through the dark?" Bill asked. "No, I mean the day. All

the days." He was eight. They searched his backpack for clues
to the inexplicable, and found *Rabbit, Run,*
his camera and journal, *Great Expectations,*
Kerouac's *Book of Dreams.* Bill asked, "When you wake from this

dream, will it be better?" Bill launched the coffin's prow
with a song: "I'm going to be perfect, starting now."

Parable of Water

We lived in an estuary of assurances
I'd just written, wry nostalgia for my boyhood—
a safe one, near a boring river. After that
first line a boy died. Not mine, but one just past the age

my safe one is, whose heart kicked its two-step dance
routine. Just this June, his name was summoned on stage
like my son's, a purple-robed high-school graduate
urged to swing into his next life, and there make good

on the promise his parents made from a few ounces
of fluent love. His next life, I understood,
is no river. Strangers laid him out on the street.
I quit writing. Then the sky floated an image:

clouds. I found his small one. Above it, his mother's—
breaking up more slowly—tracked the small cloud downriver.

The Dyer's Head

The last five years we watched Joel's ideas ripen hues
in the mild Northwest berry seasons of his hair.
Experiments with marionberry maroons,
blueberry bangs, streaks of green blackberry runner.

Teaching college, I was used to heads exploding
in new dyes week to week, like a pack of Day-Glo
kids' markers busted open. Heads deciding
to signature the air for each bright rush of the new

gusting through the centuries to change their quick lives.
They drank smoothies, and bloomed Titian blue. The pale
Apollo torso urged color on them. Joel's beliefs
arched out of the old covenant: in his spectral

mind, each strange view fruited rainbows that talked back.
When they parked him in walnut, his hair was dyed black.

Joel as Ezekiel, Singing Wheels of Fire

He had a fifties car, and fifties hair: basic black.
He could have groomed both to a wax-museum gleam
but liked his head spiky; his Plymouth Cranbrook

chugged and waddled like a fat widow. Joel felt at home
fiddling with props for the role he could not afford
to claim until he'd aged enough to let it play him

for decades. A young man fast-forwards the past, weird
trick, until it furnishes him with a history
that trues his life. Joel's Bungalow of Old Cool Records

is where I see him, fifty, building community;
serving communion, too, through loudspeakers crammed with dead
bluesmen shouting *Yeah!* at bins of antique LPs.

A white Les Paul hangs by the cash till. His gray head
hums Albert King; *Born Under a Bad Sign* puts him to bed.

Parable of Irrational Numbers

From every angle it does not solve, Joel's zero,
this hole square in the middle of the imagined
end page of a life that had so many numbers
naturally waiting to become anniversaries.

For two months Joel crossed America from one end
to the other, a pilgrim making memories
he would someday withdraw from undated chambers
of the heart, in a night of wine and smoke, to show

a lover or a son all he'd learned in that slow
pioneer drive crossing through his childhood countries—
Minnesota, Texas, Oregon. Understand:
his triangle's sum is zero. Then remember

him returning, glad—the end of his travels new—
to tell his parents: *I have so much to tell you.*

Time Trial

Prosecution's opening statement: Saint Francis,
clear the room of birds. Jesus, quit your wound display.
The poor dead we know will be forever with us

but too many jam the galleries today.
Each one can be a bird when Jesus starts his
encore Sermon on the Mount outdoors. We're in a gray

zone here: how to nail the defendant with the crime
of being jury, judge and executioner
and being nowhere and everywhere at once. Time

never answers our charges in particular
questions of murder. Time will only offer sublime
vistas of clouds. Of silent granite gardens where

victims quietly turn witness for the defense.
I enter Joel's quieted face in evidence.

Means and Ends

What's worse than dying young—scrounging roadside bottles,
fiftyish, drunk. The ex-logger canvasses the park
for barefoot hippies to buy these old running shoes.
His soles are horny, they can last until the next

good deal. He scored an antique steel gridiron, too—
know anyone old enough to prefer waffles
cooked on the burner? Each deal's the means to the next
brownbag forty of Pabst, muddying the nurse-shark

pinpoints of his eyes that guard his durable truths
against getting drunk with the adventuresome lies
meant to regale his marks and probation officer.

He'd trade skin and soul for a drink. It simplifies
my limits: I can't trade mine for Joel's lived-out youth.
"Keep those shoes on," I say, and tithe him with a dollar.

REASONS THAT REASON DOESN'T KNOW

Our nature lies in movement; complete calm is death,
wrote Pascal, and lay down with a migraine. Reason
numbs the wanderlust itching each novice beneath
the robe his vows roped him in. Footprints on the moon

spell the airless word at the end of our evening walks
where stars keep thinking *What if,* and banked roses breathe
yellow to envy of their stilled content. What stalks
this restlessness from room to room but a heart that seethes

its nomad muscle in milk our mothers expressed?
Meaning: Still the hunger that white shower feeds. Calm
the wave of thirst you want to walk on like the palm
of God, who grew new fruit far from our homes as a test.

I just checked the stars. Joel's earth is traveling still.
I go back in to Pascal, whose thought makes me ill.

PARABLE OF SLEEPWALKING

The blue-tailed skink starts and stops along the roof peak—
hunger's errand, transacted fifty times a day
fifty times higher than its six-inch-length—
alternating the spurt of habit, the stutter-step

of care. Its death is catbird-quiet in a white oak;
its lifeline consists of sugar ants on their way
through an attic window to the kitchen. The strength
of hunger aims them at some sweet spill missed by the mop.

Wake up, Rumi sang: *You're drunk, and on the edge of the roof.*
His listeners stretched prayer carpets on the sand
and believed. At night they climbed the roof and got drunk.

Most of us ground our faith one step at a time. The skink
is trying to finish lunch when the catbird lands.
Joel's heart missed a step. The catbird's song is proof.

PARABLE OF PASSOVER

In 1942 the Nazis paint a star
on the rabbi's Romanian house. His Gentile
servant brings a peasant's sheepskin coat, boots, felt hat.
He shaves beard and ringlets, kisses his two daughters

and wife—they'll die in Birkenau—and takes the fate
embodied in his firstborn son toward Israel.
In the beechwoods, a Carpathian shepherd slaughters
sheep for them. At Turkey's frontier they exit war

for a Brooklyn Talmudic shul. Decades later
an old woman rings the bell to his Viennese flat.
"I have found you," she says. "I'm dying. All your books are
safe, your clothes, your house. Here is the key. Call your son while

there's time." History needs nothing more than a pen
and air. You write it on the lampshade of your skin.

NUITES AMERICAINES

Through a glass darkly is how I saw the West was shot.
John Wayne overturned a desert rock, searched the dead
Commanche's face, and plugged his eyes. A soul cannot

track its ancestors once the lights of its death head
are burst. Movies were speed with a morphine chaser—
childhood's legal weekend drug. Then the blackness read

The End. Houselights pushed me out, the sun's eraser
rubbed out each actor's phantom life; mine, too. Day for night
is the trick filter Paul used like a hack director

to darken the role Jesus played in the white light
of one rule: love, plain and strong as the crayon sun
that lords the first page Joel drew, before movie screens

made him search out new roles projected in the flight
of illusions speeding through the eye of John Wayne's gun.

A Music Theory of Premonitions

Summer coyotes composed a pure A-minor chord
against the Grand Tetons. They loped along the lake
in concert, never altering the interval's ache
that tunes midnight to its groundnote and flattened third

and there prepares each sleeper in his mummy bag
and backpack tent for the minor apocalypse
of dreams where every daylight doubt wakes, unzips
the flimsy scrim of the body and blows like a rag

of cold mist choiring after the coyote-song.
We drove to the mountains to dissolve the city,
though the siren never quits crying emergency—
altering nothing but its voice grown wild and strong

enough to blow loose any unstaked solo tent
whose dreamer chased the one coyote running silent.

Parable of Shadows

What turns cities gray are ghosts: that's where they answer
monotonous inquiries about the future
in monotones of ash, exhaust, and verdigris.
The residue they leave is like a sustained kiss—

on this portico that sheltered one's live embrace;
on that marble sill where another leaned her face
into her arms and listened to the song of sirens
and taxis, and weighed the summer she held the reins

of a milk-paint horse, and no one called her in at dark.
The city ghosts touch gray is a moon-luminous ark,
they're its true passengers. The living are ballast,
perishables with no sure date stamped as their last.

Something stilled in them wants the facades to keep graying.
What the dead do with their colors, they're not saying.

SMOKE AND MIRRORS

I want to be honest, I tell Joel's cigarette,
and need to lie. I'm talking to a flame smaller
than the tongue of Odysseus in whatever
circle of hell made Dante, in his wool robe, shiver

in the art of telling lies for special effect:
the hardest basic lesson always, when the aim
is truths that get you tossed out by the very same
city fathers whose children will pronounce your name

with reverence once exile leaves you derelict,
then dead of some obscure fever. In my courtyard
my luck holds: my loves, my home safe, still, sequestered
from this boy's death that beats my friends' hearts too hard

for them to bear hearing each good lie I won't reject
until the coroner writes how Joel's heart got wrecked.

TIKKUN

Joel, they carved the grave turf in six pieces equal
to zones of your closed body, parts you will not use
but to stun our visits with undivided repose.
Your feet: finished dancing. They lock their long sequel

of calf and knee and thigh into fixed acknowledgment.
Your boy-god sex will never deliver a child
into your hands, those two self-taught teachers. They styled
your rainbow hair; sketched chairs, bowls, bits of craft you meant

to master in the heart's household. It was apt to break
its handiwork many times more, until mind and soul
worked out their lifelong repair in memories. These heal
worlds wounded piecemeal by love's repeated mistake:

the dream of your body outlasting your father's claim
on death first. On you, tending the cut grass of his name.

JOEL, SINGING PROVERBS

The earth is not satisfied with water. Waters
flowed over my head; I said, I am cut off.
But I was set up from everlasting, before
the earth was, when there were no depths, no fountains of
abounding water. Before mountains were settled,
before the hills I was sung forth. He had not made
the fields, the whole sum of the dust of the world.
I was there when he set a circle upon the face
of the deep, when he made firm the skies. When he gave
the sea its decree that the waters should not transgress
I knew he would bring me rain to drink in my grave.
What I have sung to you is a psalm of the grass.
We are no more divided than light from water.
Where you look, I listen. The rain has a father.

A LULLABY FOR SURVIVING

Wire grass,
creek-willow sedge
and sassafras
stanch the sunburnt edge

of evening's western coast. A catbird,
charcoal touched red, ignites the first syllable
of night's original word—
the culminating, indivisible

flame that tips each cattail's taper
to light the sky indigo. Worlds blacken
where night-words smoke the Bible paper
clouds to ash: no revising Joel back in

the light blue breath of days. Let his name anneal
my mouth. Tomorrow has other wounds to heal.

PARABLE OF LINES

Sonnets like families are a matter of lines
intersecting well or not. Unforgettable,
that's what mothers and poets want for the trouble
they push their bodies through: this creation refines

its maker's urge to make it better as it hungers
out of whichever opening birth's body made,
into this sum of unspeakable lights that have played
across the face of genesis waters longer

than even God, our firstborn, knows. Where is the face
I had before I was born? Joel should have asked this
of his mother once. That question's pain is worth the kiss
she could not answer with. Each line I erase

was a mistake of breath; another breath gets it right.
Two lines fall short here. Joel: goodnight.

THE KILIM DREAMING

Take cinnabar, indigo, alum: grind and sift
lighter than the light dust of the high summer hills.
Steep ten hours in a vat. Stir. Then, with both arms, heft
a sheep's-worth of yarn in, to soak while the night fills
with the stars of cricket-song. At dawn, boil three hours,
then wash the yarn in curd-water, water where curds
and whey are well-beaten. This aroma flowers
until you are hungry again for flatbread hard
in the sun, stuffed with fennel and peppers and chives.
From a vat of fresh water, dip enough to make
coffee. Drink its sweetened black dust. The sheep survives
the years of shearings until its feast day. Now slake
your wool in this vat. Dry it. You have Birbul's blue.
A skein of sky in your arms. A prayer come true.

1

"Sharp design, terrific colors, fine weaving, and
a bad sheep will always make a bad rug." Ahmet's
laugh can ruin a kilim. The lines of his hand
open in his shop like the first book of carpets.
This is Antalya. The Mediterranean
tiles its shore, like the blue bordering a Koran.
A twelfth-century minaret points the old town
toward heaven. Turkish, German, English, Russian—
whatever language might work—is hurled at tourists
by storefront dealers trawling for business. *Carpets!*
they hiss. They shout until the muezzin insists
on silence. A German shepherd sleeps on Ahmet's
doorstep. Step across. You won't catch Ahmet praying.
He might be reading Goethe. "Carpets," he's saying,

"attract frauds and liars, men—," he nods at the doorway,
"you shouldn't want to know your wallet, house, or heart.
I'm no missionary. I know more than I'll say
about this tribe of thieves and holy fools. To start,
distinguishing the right rug people from the wrong
begins with knowing rugs, one after another.
Shop by shop, city by city. It takes as long
as you live to tell the devil from his brother
the angel of morning. People with loose cash love
being lied to: they'll pay five times a rug's value
to believe they own the story a dealer weaves
in the air to transform his fake into their true
vacation deal. Look, fakes hang in major museums.
But some angels, like me, know how to see through them."

Once he spent three days deciding not to purchase
an antique Anatolian kilim of great
potential profit to him. "Perfect rug," he says.
"The wool was good, the design a wonder. A slight
bad feeling I had about the blue kept growing."
The dealer's boy brought apple tea on a zinc tray.
On the overstuffed divan he drank, dozed, sweating
through his shirt. Rumi sang in his ear, *Night and day*
the reed flute wants to go home to running waters.
Urging their plums and melons and mint on the world,
street vendors matched the muezzin's amplified quavers.
Under his eyelids, memories of old skies swirled
past the rug's bright idea, but its blue matched no day
he believed. "It was the wrong blue. I walked away.

"Whether you look in Baku, Konya, Yerevan,
or Istanbul's Grand Bazaar, each rug shop demands
ritual courtship. Etiquette means evasion:
the proprietor won't ask what you want. His hands
flirt with each other's clean nails. And you don't admit
all you wish, though the white walls are hung with gardens
of great birds, river willows, and stars, and each mat
underfoot proposes a heaven that pardons
any believer who lowers his head to sniff
the original dirt of the hills that is weaved
into each relic." Ahmet has a smoker's cough.
He touches his forehead. Why else has he survived
but to keep dealing paradise from his high walls?
"Are bargains what you like?" he asks. "Go someplace else."

Most visitors limit themselves to what he keeps
on the floor and walls—Caucasians, tribals. These go
for some hundreds of dollars, inscribed with the shapes
of camel hooves, goats, shepherds, emitting their glow
of unaged dyes. Ahmet sells two thousand a year
at ten percent profit. When he detects the aloof,
thorough, maddening patience of a collector,
he offers to open the first of his three safes.
If he finds the collector serious and rich
he maybe opens the second. For the rarest—
the one whom, despite business, he likes very much—
he unlocks the final safe, and hands him his test:
a rag, threadbare, four hundred years old, from Kütahya.
One who sniffs it, then bows, is fated: a buyer.

"What is a buyer? He knows wealth is paper,
an amassed abstraction." Ahmet eyes the third safe.
"Money feeds itself. With its table scraps, culture
can be bought. Like buying a baby for a wife
who is barren. You nourish it, it needs a room,
it grows on you as though you were its real father.
I have no children myself. But I know the loom
where my orphans are born is worked by a mother—,"
he gestures at his scores of rugs, "who wants to feed
her children. Who will trade her weaving, this poor child
she cannot support, to give the rest what they need."
His fingernails harrow a tribal rug's green field.
"I arrange for this child to meet you, for a fee worth
my time and your desire. I am there at the birth

of the collector: the buyer who cannot bear
confining his wealth to one orphaned rug, who has
never created a thing except cash. In here
he can amass a family. He can weave his
money through my fingers and fly home with a past,
ancient as Ararat, that confers a future
value on his fatherly care. And then, how fast
his family grows. He becomes the curator
of its private museum. He supports mothers
who live and die at their looms, and feeds their children.
A few migrate to Hamburg, work as stevedores
in his shipping business; one, maybe, is given
a chance to rise. He succeeds. The boss invites him
to his villa: there, on one wall, hangs Mother's kilim.

"When I meet someone, I'm already guessing how
not to tell him what I do. Tourists expect cheats."
Ahmet shrugs. On a cruise ship a few years ago
he was asked to bring his finer kilims, as a treat
for Americans sailing back to Athens. That night
a Long Island housewife lost a ring. "The police
presumed I'd filched it. The husband said, 'Let's indict
this bastard.' The ring was in her overnight case.
They did not apologize, and not one of them
bought a rug. They cruised away to the Parthenon
to cleanse their consciences in marble, then to swim
in hotel pools, sighing how the Turks' munitions
dump had ruined the glory of Greece. Turk rug dealers,"
Ahmet laughs, "dwell lower in hell than Greek sailors.

"But when Americans carve out the newest pit
in hell's basement, they'll call it a fallout shelter
and drag in gold and paper stocks, the hoards of shit
they vandalized the world to call theirs. They'll alter
the sign over the entryway to read, *Heaven:
Abandon all your cultures here. Be quick to show
a U.S. visa to the honor-guard Marine
bouncer at the door.*" Ahmet shakes his head. "You know,
maybe we need Dante updated. In English."
The one revenge he takes is on antique hunters
who imagine he knows no language but Turkish.
Who brag to spouses, "Watch me make this guy reverse
his dumb-ox frown, and deal." Ahmet names a price too low
for the target piece, mumbles like he doesn't know

its true worth. Lets the man walk out to strategize
and gloat to his wife. "I hold it—for special friend—,"
he'll struggle in the cheat's mother tongue. "Please,
tomorrow? Here again?" He'll delay his deft end-
game for days, then—the morning he sees the checkbook
in the man's hand—announce: "Remember, you thought me
an idiot? You were planning to make me look
small to your wife. A fool. I'm a fool who speaks three
languages and understands four more. And this piece
you wish to steal is great, I congratulate you
on your eyes. It is for sale, and at a good price.
Only not to you. Never to you. Its value
lies beyond arrogant pricks like you in this life."
The man gapes. Ahmet winks at his smiling wife.

 2

The boy who found some slight success in Germany
was brother to Ahmet's father. A childless man,
he wired home: *Bring your son here and teach him to see*
what he may do with a German education.
He also wired train fare for Ahmet's family.
A job, possibly, in the shipping magnate's firm?
Ahmet's father was convinced. When they left Turkey
he sang to Ahmet, "My Anatolian worm,
don't cry, one day you will grow wings made of Deutschemarks.
You'll bang your head against Nietzsche and whistle Brahms."
He dreamed aloud: the nice house they'd own, city parks
for their picnics. Ahmet's uncle failed to meet them
at the station. The police had found a copy
of the telegram in his fist, in an alley.

"Shot once in the head," the sergeant tapped his temple.
"Like so. We found no pistol. And yet his wallet
was untouched." The answer the family wanted was simple
and not to be had; further inquiries would kill it.
So they accepted official condolences,
the coroner's report, the dead man's clothes and cash.
Ahmet's father, gray-faced, entered the loose census
of Turks loading German ships. Mother took in wash.
Ahmet was burdened with his uncle's books—Hegel,
Schopenhauer, a dog-eared Rumi and Hikmet—
and an ex-Nazi headmaster who liked to regale
his flock, these goat-children of guest-workers, with pet
theories about what might have been, had the Third Reich
prevailed: "Little Atatürks," he snapped, "you'd be rich."

Ahmet speaks better German than Turkish. He left
his parents pressing shirts in the laundry they bought
with the pension his father won after the lift
failed on a dockside hoist. He had been taught
by Marxist lecturers that in a strong workers'
democracy the rights of all would be upheld—
including East German refugees and shirkers
too slow to outrun a crate falling from nets filled
with tons of Turkish wool. The father would never
walk again; the son would get the education
his uncle's death required. He had heard them sever
their past from his future as a European—
they confined their prayers to the whispery bedroom,
then emerged to talk bad kitchen-German with him.

"It was winter, final exams. I lived on coffee
and Wittgenstein, one room with an empty white wall.
And kept looking up from books, toward it. I'd see
those long terrible sophistries, magnified all
out of proportion, float their print across its face
and melt away. As though failing to describe God's
body, the earth's great secret. The wall would erase
each word like the breath of a shadow. I threw wads
of paper blackened with more jargon per square inch
than the worst scholar, and the wall batted them down.
Resisted foreign logic. I felt the wall cinch
its Turkish knot in my heart: *You're no more German
than my white is a color.* The next day I bought
my first kilim, for it. 'School,' I told it, 'is out.'"

Imagine that boy, Wittgensteined out of his mind,
seeing a Neolithic goddess manifest
on cold blank Heidelburg plaster. She's as blind
to his waking dream as he to his long-suppressed
Anatolia of dervish and cicada,
black Türkmen tent and Alexander's white chiton,
this land like the head of a mare galloping from Asia
to quench its thirst in the Mediterranean—
imagine him apprehending hell's granite-gray
German winter, the voluminous abstractions
inking his chill fingers, while in the kilim, May
dyes a plateau beneath Ararat with fractions
of madder and indigo the goddess revealed
to a woman setting up her loom in a field.

In the dream emanating from the wall's white screen
the kilim-goddess filtered color like hashish
through Ahmet's discontent, and gave him unreason:
an itch to plunge his hands in wool wet with *abrash*
of oak gall and walnut husk, pomegranate rind
and cochineal; to recover, body and soul,
the geometrical infinities refined
through the centuries of weaving he'd seen his whole
lost boyhood ago in houses where village girls
reassembled the goddess in slit tapestry
for their dowries; he could almost feel their secret curls
shedding the myrrh of sex in his palm. He was young and horny
and homesick after fourteen winters of *Kultur:*
he wanted to be a kilim-philosopher.

His mother sold two mosques to put him in business.
This was the family joke, earned after her tears.
Ladik prayer rugs, their *mihrabs* triple arches,
passed from mother to daughter some two hundred years.
"My venture capital," he smiles, the smile rigid,
archaic. The smile knows she sold a heritage
to permit her one son's homecoming to succeed
in this shop he shrugs off as "my mess of pottage."
There was a daughter, too. His sister, dead at birth.
She passed blind through those triple gates to paradise.
Her stillborn dowry gave Ahmet this place on earth.
Once he prospered, he tracked down—for ten times the price—
the first heirloom; that fall, he buried his mother.
He prays on it, one prayer: to find the other.

"So I am better equipped," he says, "than some men
to appraise these works from women's hands that keep me
accustomed to good food and cars. I'm forty-nine,
I'll never marry. The weavers—whose rugs you see
and walk all over and idly finger—they're my
harem, in one sense, because I pay top dollar
for traditional design and natural dye.
They can buy a TV and refrigerator
if they wish. Their men don't spend the days drinking tea,
they milk the goats, chop wood, reap in place of their wives
at harvest, since the wives weave their prosperity.
I'm married to hundreds of these family lives.
And to my BMW M6, sure. But in each weaver
I see my sister in heaven. And my mother.

"Maybe I learned this seeing from the Nemesis
in our Antalyan museum. She always stares past
her onlooker. Where else is fate, if not the space
opening behind you? It's like the ocean mist
when you face these Toros Mountains, then mountain fog
if you turn to the Mediterranean night.
Ask archeologists: however deep you dig
to bring the oldest known levels of ruin to light,
there's another layer underneath. It's a story
you could hear from the face that leans over your deep
slit trench. A girl, quiet. She could be a moon fairy.
Then she giggles: 'Is that your grave? Or can't you sleep?'"
Ahmet's thumb jerks. The photo hangs behind him. Hers.
Her loom in a field. This is what he remembers.

Like any village girl, she's a walking garden—
scarf, blouse, enveloping *salvar*, all floral, each
a clashing season. He'd been clued to a hidden
kilim in this mosque, an antique scrap within reach
under decades of votive rugs. Of course a price
had not been named. He handed over enough cash
to educate ten boys, lifted each rug twice,
found nothing. A tall voice says: *If you had one wish,*
where would it be? On his knees, he looks up. Blue eyes,
steady, assured. Hadn't he locked the door? "I'd ask
where my mother went," she says. "Everyone here lies."
She scuffs a floorboard with one sandal. Not a task
for Hercules. The scrap beneath justifies all.
How can he repay her? The eyes glaze, like blue tile.

She wants to sit at the wheel of his turquoise car.
Where is the key? Which pedal makes the speed? She wants
to learn. More than that: to leave. The floral wear
looks strained on her, it can't contain her impatience.
She finds the automatic lock, and presses hard.
"So drive," he laughs. The village boys surround them now,
faces in skull caps, silently mouthing a word,
a leer, vanishing when it meets his stare. "We go,"
she pleads in English. A sharp command outside yanks
the boys back. The imam stands at Ahmet's window
beckoning, with a cartload of kilims. "The thanks
of God and our women," he bows. "Take this black widow.
These were her mother's." Dazed, Ahmet obeys. He dumps
them in the trunk. The girl blasts the horn. The imam jumps.

On the road out, she snakes into the back, rolls down
a window, releases the scarf. In his mirror
it flails, a severed wing. The salvar balloon
in the exhaust, the blouse. She's in jeans, a halter,
singing, "You are my chauffeur, take me to the west!"
Past the last field where village women might see him
he brakes. "Tourist yachts stop in Alanya, you pest,"
he barks. "Maybe a dockside pimp can make your dream
come true. Or you can try the police. Tell me why
I shouldn't drop you in their laps." "Unlock the trunk,"
she tells him, "please. Open the trunk. I will not lie,
I will show you a better reason to get drunk
than that old rag you found." In the mirror, now, she
seems taller. "Get out," he says. Then hands her the key.

She unrolls rug after rug on the Mercedes,
draping windshield and hood. The first few, typical
for here—stepped-diamond dazzles, sawtooth selvages,
tomato-red fields filled with stacked horizontal
deltas. Boring. But nice abrash. They have some age,
perhaps—and no chemical dyes. But the next rug
is like finding, rolled in the daily news, one page
of a Koran long lost. It's a visible drug.
He controls himself. "It's not Anatolian,"
he says. "I've seen one similar Kazak. But this
star-medallion, these greens—Persian?" "Circassian,"
she says. "Like me." The word strikes him the way a kiss
changes everything. "Before I show you the rest,
you should know—," the blue eyes narrow, "this is no test."

In his trade, he has met Europeans who talk
of blind wine tastings, time-trials for the nose and tongue—
he's glad he's not on trial. Each kilim makes him weak
with speculation. She's taken him on a long
migrant swath—Ottoman Aleppo, the Czarist
century of Daghestan, remnants of Kurd,
Seljuk, Türkmen, Mongol—beneath it all, like schist
underlying good grape vines, an unspoken word.
It could be *sex*—he has decided she's twenty,
maybe older. He's thirty-three, the Jesus-age,
earthly male perfection. Her rugs say, *Marry me.*
But she stands apart from them like another page,
an end-page. Whatever was once written there is
torn. But is, he feels, the question of a princess.

"Your mother's dead?" he asks. She has reached the last three
of twelve kilims. Six could be worth six months' sharp trade;
three might fetch far more at auction. He'll phone Sotheby's.
He could set her up with a sea view and a maid.
As though she approves his plan, she's nodding. "Dead? Yes.
I hope so. She's not the woman I buried here.
That was my wet nurse. No, my shield, my Artemis—
she did steal me from death. And she might save me once more
if you sell these without stealing my share." She grows
more strong-minded by the hour. It's not time to share
his scheme—these last rugs could be best. Or worst, who knows?
"Enough for now," she nods. "You'll see when we get there."
Where? Does his face teleprompt all he leaves unsaid?
"Antalya." She's in the car. "I want my own bed."

Far back as stories go, beauty like hers was sold
to kings of this hill or that oasis, to gain
fair skin, eyes like heaven's tile. Coin-belted with gold,
shawled with silver, child-brides caravanned off to reign
over tribes of black sheep or silkworms and bear sons
with skin like Venice or Rome, the better to trade
silk, wool, spice, for spun glass, imperial steel. Crones
of their own tongue flanked them. The loaded camels swayed,
three days' journey unveiled a far country, finished
with oil to anoint their nakedness for some khan
unbuckling his sword. Whatever these pale queens wished
was theirs for a blue-eyed son. This ancient bargain
earned afternoons at the women's loom, to grieve
lost homes, fields, and borders warped against the goddess-weave.

Odysseus and Penelope, then, are one.
The story of the nomad princess is the thing
lost, save in her personal tapestries undone
by daily use, worn to fragments by her kneeling
to pray for deliverance. Her words stay secret;
the language her fingers knot is loss made visible,
coded in calyx and oak-leaf, dyes of regret.
A goddess with bull-horn arms grips the twin eagles
tribal khans and caesars will claim for their emblem.
Flowers strict as compasses radiate in all
directions where she's no longer free to seek them—
the same flowers that defined her mother's tent wall.
Decades abstract the designs her sorrows cannot say. . . .
This is what she tells Ahmet on the coast highway.

After this parable, she crashes. He bears her
sleeping weight rolled up in its opiate fatigue,
leaves her on his bed. It is as though his sister
or mother made young had returned from death. Each rug
he hauls in the shop writes one stanza in the lives
of women locked in lyric patterns of closure—
lines of queens who die far from home, whose dyes survive
their dispossession, and change death into treasure.
Ahmet eyes the last three kilims, still rolled and twined.
Tomorrow's bargaining with her might go better
with a preview. And if she had this trick in mind,
is this her test? Stow them by the bed, then. Let her
keep her promise. Let her keep them close. There's a heap
of tribal rugs near the front door: maybe he'll sleep.

Of course he dreams. He's a long thread spun from gut-silk,
coiled in a reed basket. Whatever he touches
connects to other spidery fingers. Moon-milk
pours down on black tents where crones are weaving stretches
of pasture and streams. From the streams, grass weaves willows,
the willows weave moonlight into a snowy hill
shaped like a drop-spindle, a teardrop mosque. Snows
fatten into wool, wool shears off in clouds that fill
the crones' spider-hands: piles of roving plied at wheels
humming, whispering, mountain springs fed by snowmelt.
Girls' laughter ripples through a field of chamomile.
The earth is spun, seasons woven, moon-warp, weft of gilt
summer. The landscape shakes. . . . A hand on his shoulder:
"Coffee," she laughs. "Before I get any older."

"You had The Dream," she nods when he's done with coffee
and story. "One part of it. More may come later.
It's a woman's dream. I knew one man who could see
what you saw last night—a eunuch with no daughter
or son, an old dyer who roamed with the Qashqai.
He told it to my nurse Leila when I was six.
I can see his hands, stained with indigo mash. Why
did the dream pick you?" He shrugs. The turquoise eyes fix
on his face like a developing photograph.
Around them, the noise of the bazaar—hammered tin,
sewing machines, haggling over fruit. "More than half
of you may be your mother. You may be less man
than you'd like. But more angel, strange as that must seem.
Come." She stretches. "It's time to see the waking dream."

She unties the first, and rolls it out on the bed.
Three compartments filled with *elma,* circles of eight
apples, linked by diagonals of silver thread.
A smaller compartment in the core of each great
field of espaliered apples holds the goddess,
headless, strong-armed, her infinitely repeated
body-diamond stuffed with a cross, a lightning-S
like *tai chi,* or an axe-head lozenge. She's bordered
with thorn-trellises, more apples. He's on the verge
of a name, he can taste it in the apricot
and olive and apple-red abrash, and his surge
toward utterance is like seeing the black knot
of hair between a woman's legs opening there,
on his bed. The name won't come. He exhales clenched air.

"Reyhanli," she says, as his tongue dissolves the knot.
"You'd think you'd never seen one before. Put your hand
here—," she guides his wrist down, "this one goddess is not
made of wool. The weaver had broken a command
of her husband and was about to die. She had
an old nurse cut off her hair. That night they wove this.
The wing design, here? Feel it. That's gold wire, not thread,
and a dove's feathers. The price of a Christian kiss,
Leila told me. The weaver was no longer young
but age did not kill her desire—her husband did."
Ahmet feels the twisted gold garrotes, tufts of wing.
"Not a village weaver, then?" he asks. "Leila said,
'Child, she is you a hundred years ago—a queen
who should have killed the king. You will see what I mean.'"

As though the rug is rising up against his palm
Ahmet steadies himself. This room where he has made
love to girls is levitating. Animal calm
suffuses her face. What force is being displayed
here, what needles his hand as though to brocade it
to the kilim? —that any minute now might soar
and fly him dizzily eastward, to the shallow pit
where such a woman is being strangled as a whore.
Where is the orphan who annoyed him in that mosque?
Her village disguise flew out his car window. He
is bent over, she's above him, something's at risk
in this transaction, he cannot even foresee
one minute of his future now. And she sees this.
"Fresh air," she suggests, "a stroll by the water." Yes.

Mediterranean glare. "I should know your name,"
Ahmet begins, shielding his eyes. "My name? Today
it's Ana. Once it was Nani. Then Nana. Same
girl, different ages. I was born Anane."
She works her toes into fine quartz pebbles that sand
a hotel's beach. Ahmet's tribals furnish its rooms.
Coming here has helped him close tough deals that opened
in his shop; here, the spark of feeling in charge chimes
against sea-sparkle that spreads like all the silver
he has taken through the years. There is more to take.
"Anane," he says: "*tradition.*" "Or, *from mother
to daughter,*" Ana replies. "It was a headache
to hear—when Leila was in a fury with me
or my mother's vanishing." She glares at the sea.

"There was a pilot. God knows how and where they met.
I was three. Leila said I would call him *Nato.*
He could balance me over his head on the flat
of his palm, and I'd spread my arms and shout *We go!*
That's all I learned. One morning my father was found
dead inside his tent. He was Kurdish, a big khan.
Mother was gone. His sisters claimed she'd fed him ground
glass. Then there was a boat in the night on Lake Van,
just Leila and those rugs and me. I was wrapped in
that Reyhanli you saw. Leila sang lullabies.
'Anane,' she sang, 'may you never be trapped in
a man's tent like that. But you have your mother's eyes.'
There was no moon. A jet roared far above, red lights
winking. Leila told me I cried *We go!* that night."

62

A man in a swimsuit jogs past them, a girl
balanced like a tiny surfboard above his head.
Waist-deep he stops: "Okay, baby, fly!" With a squeal
she's launched into the blue. "So once your father died,"
Ahmet asks, "why did Leila take off with you?" "She
was dead otherwise," Ana says. "Maybe me, too.
We had no Turkish law, it wasn't a city—
tents and sheep, men who wore bandoliers. They'd shoot you
from horseback if you crossed their pastures. Leila saw
two heads dumped from saddlebags, once. Turkish police.
They'd burnt the car, with the bodies. There was no law
but my father's blood. Leila would have paid the price
on my mother's head. And for good reason. Her skill
included recipes for sending men to hell."

Ahmet understands the dizzying touch the rug
exerted this morning—a touch like the onset
of some undetectably fatal dose, a drug
served in a pilaf by practiced hands. He should get
away, give back these kilims, rise up, run. His legs
are heavy, his arms. "What was it?" he asks. "Hemlock,"
Ana says. Her fingers sift quartz. "Brewed in the dregs
of his coffee. It isn't a relic of Greek
democracy. Socrates swallowed what women
like Leila distilled in women's silence as long
as they have woven. Was Leila an Amazon?
Believe it. She could kill with a sheep-gut string
or cup of milk. For Mother—for herself—she killed.
Stones thrown to kill me she intercepted, my shield."

She takes his palm, wraps it around both of her fists.
"Those village boys," she says, "ambushed me. Rocks this size,
meant for my head. Leila was the reason they missed.
I stepped out one evening, a rock flew past my eyes.
Leila pushed me down in the dooryard, threw herself
over me. Stones thumped her back like a drum. 'Old witch!'
they yelled, 'you want to die too?' She howled like a wolf
among dogs. Somehow she got up. 'The one I catch,'
she screamed, 'will not be the last to see his own blood
in the dirt.' She kept a razor on her necklace—
maybe they saw it flash. They ran. 'Help me inside,
Nani,' she said. 'Call the imam. I spit in his face,
but I can make him swear to keep you safe until
the angel comes.' You," Ana says. "You're the angel."

Leila had paid a letter-writer to mail him
the clue about the kilim-fragment in the mosque.
"What she knew," Ana says, "concerned how the imam
was instructing his house-boy at night in the task
of male pleasure. It was meant to be our ticket
out of there. Another letter—for the police—
was our security." She pats her jeans pocket.
"I still might use it. The imam took her advice.
She did not let herself die until he had sworn
his oath and gone. She said a rock had burst her spleen.
At the end, she said, 'Anane, you cannot mourn.
You will go. There can be no other medicine.'"
Ana touches his arm. "Leila will send a dream.
We have to be ready. And I must find a loom."

Hypnotized by stories, Ahmet dogs her quickened
pace through shop crowds—almost, he recalls, like trailing
his mother home from market, his small fist in her hand.
There seems to be no end to the things he's failing
to foresee. He's simply an agent—an angel,
she said?—of whatever next thing a dead woman
has in mind for the two of them. As though he fell
out of a world where he was used to looking down,
and looking up from some midpoint of that free-fall
is no longer able to tell the difference
between future and past, heaven and earth, angel
and woman, man, animal, waters, rocks and plants.
Back inside the shop, he feels he's about to drown.
She lays out the next kilim: "Why don't you lie down?"

Nothing has prepared him for an object this old.
Or else everything has, but with unaccustomed
velocity. This stark kilim's six arches weld
two reds and one blue into a lullaby hummed
by the centuries. "Four hundred years," Ana says,
"this has been traveling toward you. You are safe.
You can lie down." Although it feels sacrilegious,
he does. It stops the room's spinning. He is the waif,
the orphan in some temple, now. She's returning
yesterday's favor, the rescue from murderous
boys. As he drifts off, he imagines she's turning
into what she will be, or always was, ageless
expert, guided by unseen hands. His Rolodex
is in her hands, his phone. His life, which she protects.

Dreamlessness. Sleep like an axe that severs his head
full of confusion from the body's self-repair.
Morning, still, when he wakes. Which morning? It feels good,
that's all. It could be any morning. The first. There
she is, Ana. In a chair. "Welcome back," she says.
"You slept four centuries. Who are Havva, Hamdi,
Fatma?" He blinks three times. "Please don't tell me I was
talking in sleep." "No," she laughs, "the embroidery
behind your desk. It has your name, too." His mother,
father, and stillborn sister. He narrates his life
for her. He has all morning. And sometime after
he will do the next thing she asks. "You have no wife,"
Ana says at last. "A man married to kilims.
Ready to go? I found yarn," she says. "For the loom."

~ 4 ~

Northwest they drive, into the Yuntdag, *horse mountains.*
Three thousand feet up, wild pistachio trees dot
ridges like old horse-teeth, overgrazed barrens.
A women's weaving co-op—how has Ahmet not
heard of it?—is rooted in twenty villages
connected by donkey paths, a few gravel roads.
Now in truth he is her chauffeur. She manages
him like the baby the princess finds in the reeds,
and somehow he trusts this wry reversal of roles
he fantasized on their first drive, along the coast.
A master dyer awaits them among these hills.
The way is mapped in Ana's head. She says, at most,
"Left here." Much of the drive her eyes stay closed. Ana,
he guesses, is taking directions from Leila.

Evening. Flatbread and tea in the dyer's stone house.
Two grandmothers are preparing Ahmet's pallet.
Ana's gone. A tent has been set up for her use
higher up. The loom's ready. "I'll need your wallet,"
she said when they arrived. "We may be here a week
or more. There are weavers whose work is worth knowing.
You'll find your camera and a favorite book
or two. You'll know when it's time to find me." Growing
inside him, like the flame in the kerosene lamp,
a regret: that she is preparing a distance
she'll soon resume. Her touch felt like an airmail stamp
on his forehead, fingers moistened by her lips once,
twice, three times. Then she turned and joined the dyer
at the door. But sleep will cool regret's low fever.

Waking, he finds Rumi, and a bowl of goat-milk.
A dried poppy marks the page: *In the slaughterhouse
of love, they kill only the best, none of the weak
or deformed,* he reads. *Don't run away from this
dying. Whoever's not killed for love is dead meat.*
How many times must he be reborn? Already
once, in the vigil she kept in the wooden seat
beside his kilim-bed. Here, too, his male body
stretches beneath him in a numb drowse, like the husk
of a cicada clamped to tree-bark. Floating, he
appraises its shell, topped by a funeral mask
he knows from the shaving mirror. . . . It was the tea
she tricked him with. Dried poppies. Which morning is it?
A knock, outside. The weavers want him to visit.

An hour later, alert—the bowl of milk aroused
his animal health; yet another recipe
from Leila's hoard?—, he's inspecting carpets warehoused
in a new stone shed, raking knotted piles brusquely,
betraying no trace of interest: a dealer
again, expert from his eyes to his fingertips.
Several dozen are good. He'll place an order—
soon. Why do these women smile? One covers her lips
with one hand. With the other, she plucks his wallet
from a waist-pouch. "Anane said you might need this."
The low current of laughter is friendly. Ahmet
shrugs, shakes his head and joins in. Ana does not miss
a trick in her shadowy plan to throw him off
his guard. This is love's slaughterhouse. She is the knife.

"Then you must know where she is. When I can see her,"
he says, once they've fixed the terms of their agreement—
once he has accepted the fact that these weavers
bargain as one, backed by their husbands' trust. "Her tent
will be your tent soon," the same woman says. "Not yet.
She sends these words for you: Breathe easy and sleep well."
She remains after the rest, taking a hint, file out.
"This afternoon we're picking pistachios to sell
in Bergama. The village will be empty. The men
are gone to the plains to harvest tobacco, grapes,
cotton. If you wish, you'll find their teahouse open.
Forgive me, there is one more thing. Here." She unstraps
the pouch from her belt, and leaves. A leaf of paper
lies inside, wrapped around a folding razor.

This was Leila's first and last weapon. When she was
young and beautiful, it defended her against
a drunk British sailor at the Dardanelles.
In Atatürk's battle for Sakarya, August
1921, it cut the throat of a Greek
officer who threatened her mother. Other men
have felt its bite. Leila told me it would speak
one word most men could not bear to hear a woman
pronounce. She would have waved it at you, too, seeing
the desire you carried with me to bed, that first
night in Antalya. Now its reason for being
what it was is done. You knew there would be a test
we both must pass. What divides us may keep you safe.
Unfold it. He does. A basil leaf, scored in half.

The stem scarcely holds the halves together. He lifts
blade and leaf to smell the hand that plucked it. Then reads:
Maybe I cannot stop receiving Leila's gifts
with this kilim. Maybe it is all her death needs.
I will not know until I have woven both sides
whether this rug will match us like lost twins. Leila
may send a stronger, second dream—one that divides
me forever. But half will always be Ana,
for you. That part is done with Leila's razor.
A few more nights will show me what I have to see,
my angel. My hand trembles. I can write no more.
The message prays itself twice, three times, silently
in his head, forming a strong warp through which his own
wishes float their wefts and knots, weaving blood to bone.

The shed's close air grows stale. He heads to the teahouse,
nervous with hope, and thirsty. It is not empty.
He is washing a coffee urn when the dry hiss
comes at him from an unlit corner: "There's raki
here. For the big rug-dealer who uses his brains
to make women rich. Bring a glass." On the table
beside the half-empty bottle, a pair of canes
point at Ahmet's stomach like the broken barrel
of a shotgun. Behind them, a lean figure propped
on elbows over a cup. "I suppose my wife
didn't speak of me," it says. "But I hear you dropped
a shitload of cash in her lap. Fine for her. Life
says, Drink whatever poison God puts before you,
some of it is sweet. Mine's enough for one or two."

Ahmet touches his forehead, takes a chair. "No glass?"
the man observes, "then no friend. Fine. An enemy
makes a better target. Let me drink to your ass,
which the bitches are kissing. That's over for me."
The cripple's drunk. It would be no insult to go
without a word. "I was a woodcutter. My axe
could still split you in half. I can't swing it, you know—
fall on my own ass then. But I'm not in your fix.
You're not married, but you think you can get away
with it. Not true. I divorced that witch,"— the woman
with the pouch, Ahmet guesses—"divorced her the day
she talked the rest into voting for damnation,
this woman-only thing. The men should have backed me."
He empties the cup. "Their heads are full of pussy."

The drunk's menace is toothless but gossipy, sly.
Ahmet feels safe enough to whet his interest.
"You mean their co-op?" he asks. "Isn't that why
the men are working, instead of doing their best
to stay drunk?" He pings the bottle for emphasis.
The women have shown him how willing the men were
to change work habits to build this new cash business.
"Cash means electricity, televised soccer
in here," Ahmet gestures. "Who knows? Even you might
thank them for that." The cripple barks, "I would thank you
to fetch your little whore, and fuck her for me, right
here," and slams his cup. The razor says its word, *No,*
in Ahmet's hand. He flings both canes to the far wall.
"Snakes can't walk," he snaps, leaving. "I won't watch you crawl."

His fling with violence leaves him shaken. There must
be more bastards, a gang no one mentions, teenage
pricks from the next village. He wants to find them, fight
through what the drunk woodcutter provoked—this male rage
that makes him finger the razor in his pocket
and stride uphill, searching. Ana can't be alone,
he wants to surround her like radar. He'll make it
clear, she needs a new shield, a man to stop the stone
aimed at her. He's running now, briars claw his pants,
beggar-lice grab at his sleeve. An oak-root trips him,
his hip strikes rock. Leila will not keep her distance:
No, she's making the whole hill say, *no farther.* Shame
overtakes rage. What can he do? Spent, pained, rueful—
he could use a drunkard's cane now—he limps downhill.

5

A dish of pistachios, olives, and white cheese
has been left in his room. A samovar, still warm,
honey, fresh clothes laid out on his pallet. Rumi's
open to a new page: *You are granite. I am*
an empty wine glass. You know what will happen when
we touch—he reads the rest, about reason, patience,
passion. He washes, changes, eats, drinks tea, lies down.
Apart from his unreasonable impatience
the wait makes sense. Let her tent come downhill to him
inside his closed eyes. Let him not try to find her
otherwise. Maybe Leila aimed half of the dream
at him, at the stillborn half that was his sister.
Madder of earth, indigo of sky. Where they meet
beneath his eyelids, a tremor reaches his feet:

An earthquake levels his shop of two-story brick.
Only kilims, *he sings,* cannot fall. *Looms explode*
like overstrung harps, springs burst out of his wall clock.
Corpses swell with cholera in the red rubble God
kicks around in a seismic tantrum. One rug
endures stones and spilled vitals. It lies low, rescued
by him. He is a looter: to get rich he'll dig
through pretzeled pipe, plaster smash, the battered, half-nude
sprawl of a girl's torso protecting the kilim.
Fine, *he sings,* fine for me. You got the wrong answer
to your petition, no one's spared. *With the sharp shim*
of a plank, he pries Ana's hands off his treasure,
rolls it up, hurries away. He's executed
at the first checkpoint. Two cops seize what he looted.

Now he's a cop. His partner lies in an alley.
With shuttle and yarn, he draws a murder report
that shows the partner—his uncle?—in a volley
of bullets from his gun. He designs the next part,
it's the car the killer drives—Fiat, no, Audi,
no, he's brocading the Mercedes coupe he'll buy
with this bundle pinned to the street beneath his knee.
It's nightfall. His throat is cut. He stares at the sky,
the kilim flies overhead in a shipping trunk
for Germany. A boy is awaiting it there,
Ahmet the little Atatürk, the image-drunk
believer ready to kill and die to acquire
paradise—this rag the size of a girl beaten
to death in the earthquake drawn by the rug's pattern.

Terrific pressure on his throat. Not dreaming, now.
Something heavy grunts on his chest. He grabs smooth wood,
a cane—pushes, gulps. The woodcutter hisses, "How
do you like it with a man on top?" He is dead,
the cripple's arm-strength tremendous, the black-out veil
falling. Then the weight topples, the cane lifts. A wraith
hovers. Beside his head, a gurgling, like a pail
of milk tipped over in the dark room, and his breath
comes back in gags as though he's swallowing iron.
The wraith kneels. "Do not die," it's whispering. Long hair
brushes his face. Ana. No, the other woman,
the woodcutter's ex-wife. In her hand, a razor.
"Breathe," she says. "Yes. Stay still. The others will come soon."
She floats through the doorway. Beyond her, a horned moon.

He obeys. Beside him, the dead thing he should be
lies prostrate, blind eyes targeting the moon, the spill
of jugular dye diked within the outflung V
the arms shape. An offering. Sacrificial pool
the goddess drinks. Ahmet kicks at its withered leg
and the doorway darkens. Their calm is Amazon,
their quiet speed: the corpse rolled into a frayed rug,
shouldered out like mutton, shovelfuls of salt thrown
upon the blood to soak it up. "We'll treat the goats
to that," a voice jokes. The shovel blade rasps the floor.
The dead man's wife kneels down again. "Funeral rites
tomorrow. Brain stroke, see? You dropped the dyer's
pot of cochineal." She smiles. "You should have killed him
in the teahouse. Don't argue. Hush. Ana will come."

Nearness of death is deathly enough: lassitude
after the adrenal flood, the near-surrender.
After the blood-stink stupor and burial squad,
vague drift and ache. Then surfacing to an odor,
poignant, green. A voice, fading in: " . . . to be in such
a passionate adoration—," Basil. A moth
in his hair. Reach for it. A hand is there. "I pitch
my tent in the sky. . . . " His head's in her lap, her mouth
lullabying. Reach higher. Reach to her cheek: wet
cool. His searching touch lowers her eyes, to search his.
He blinks a tear, hers. "Ahmet," she weeps, "my granite.
If you had died I would kiss your headstone. Like this."
A curtain of wet hair, basil. He tries to speak
through crushed granite. Mothwing lips, lighting on his cheek.

6

A woman, naked, pouring milk. There are no men
for miles in the night, no man alive but one, stretched
on his side in a candle's amniotic, wan
halo, asleep again. A cup of goat's milk, enriched
with white drops squeezed from the head of a flower,
squeezed in threes through vertical slits, as she was taught.
She stirs in honey, cinnamon. In half an hour
she'll wake him, and raise his head. The man will forget
nothing they have done, but will sleep until restored,
days, until his bruised ribs mend, his swollen throat clears.
It is the story of his last dream—the whispered
end of one world, its mothwing words beating in her ears—
and of the fever named Ana, who must reconcile
twin dreams on one loom. She warms milk with the candle.

Some marriages do not last long: a mayfly span.
A bridge of kisses over the depth of one night.
The lover crosses over, keeps climbing, even
when the night's uphill path resolves nothing. Her feet
move to the muted music of the weft shuttle
in the open tent devoted to a nomad
will. It lets her memorize the urge to settle,
in guard borders of trellised fruit grown to divide
love's momentary garden from the world where men
buy rugs like wives, exotic, to adorn their homes
and magnify their height on the rug's prostration.
Where the infinite urge to inhabit love rhymes
with its endless negative image: to go
outside it, far through all women alone can know.

So she settles herself at the loom, Anane,
patient, listening to the country of cricket
and nightingale. Her kilim has begun to say
what she once was: orphan princess in the pocket
of a khan, deserted by a mother who longed
for one horizon so well she found a pilot.
The jet-black skies of her Lake Van crossing are thronged
with flashes of red goodbye, eight-rayed stars that knot
childhood to the song *We go.* Violet axe-heads
repeat what Leila did to the boy who raped her
in an apricot grove. Bandoliers *X* that dead
cipher, her father. The imam's virile member,
an arrowed swastika. All backgrounded by the blue
of her eyes. Each image infinite, wrenched, and true.

Leila lies underneath: the tight warp of black wool
that hugs the male images close, and wrings their necks.
The black moon's release, the full moon's pull.
Each earth-tremor is passed through her, Leila who plucks
the zither, the dead dove's feathers, and the girl-child
out of one blood-ruled world, back into an older
law, immeasurable, silent: the goddess-willed
original night that surrounds each green bower
where she survives male-ordered histories, and codes
messages in root and leaf, grain and wool and howl
of wolf in heat. The crickets transmit her passwords,
the nightingales improvise her night-long hymnal,
and Ana knows that Leila's dream has bypassed her—
as she wished—for this man who must be her brother.

In the eye-blue field that centers her early life,
she starts brocading Ahmet's earthquake-dream, the end
of his weird, unreasoned, self-killing knot of strife.
It looks like a prophecy she cannot defend
him against. She cannot defend what she will do
once she completes this apocalyptic torment
and his first dream, translating creation anew—
that weave of willows and waters from the black tent
of the goddess's mountain-body. His car key
sleeps in her pouch; the blue Mercedes will be worth
less than what he can earn from the twelve kilims she
is leaving him—weaves that smother her in the earth
of her past. Despite Leila's order, she will mourn.
And like her mother, take the horizon's medicine.

 7

Lot three: this pristine specimen is Reyhanli,
mid-nineteenth century. The fine execution
of three trellis borders and the field's sandikli,
or dowry chests, indicates a Circassian
provenance. Near ancient Antioch—Antâkya,
in tourist Turkey—the village Reyhanye
supplied Ottomans in Aleppo (now Syria)
with such kilims as townhouse drapes and portières.
White wool warps and wefts. Undyed cotton forms the white
designs; generous use of silver and gold threads.
Unique accents include rare feathers. The highlight,
stunningly long silver hair—from a woman's head,
it's safe to presume. Bidding starts at nine thousand.
The gentleman in blue. Thank you, I see your hand.

Lot four: this composition of six arches will,
no doubt, strike some here as plain, not to say austere,
with its palette of red and blue. Archetypal
in its resemblance to wall paintings—I refer
to Mellaart's The Goddess From Anatolia—
at Çatal Hüyük, dated 5900 BC,
it compresses a span of eight millennia.
Best carbon-14 guess is fifteenth century.
Tradition describes it as a saf, six mihrabs
for family prayer. Whether the deity you
prefer is Allah or Cybele, nothing robs
this rug's pure power of madder and indigo.
The reserve is thirty thousand pounds. Good luck in
not envying the pleasure of the one who wins.

∾ 8 ∾

"Disillusionment? Yes," Ahmet winces. "Half-true."
He emerged from that last long sleep in the Yuntdag,
Ana and Mercedes gone. Not even a few
words of scribbled goodbye to preserve the aura
encompassing his time with her. The radiance
in his chest became an ordinary hurt, bruised
ribs, and what tightened his throat was not the lost chance
at a future she represented, then revised
into a past briefer than a kiss: just muscles
on the mend. The woodcutter's widow led him up
the hill. He limped with one cane, she parted tangles
of briar with the other. Pointed it at the top
of the tent. "There," she said. "It's yours." It hurt to laugh.
At least she hadn't lied. He took a photograph.

It hid in plain sight, a high pasture. "We can go,"
he told her, and turned. "You don't have to sleep in there,"
she answered, "but don't refuse what's coming to you.
I will wait below. Do you still have that razor?
You will need it." A parting joke. He has not shaved
for days. Maybe the women hope he'll cut his throat
to cover the woodcutter's killing; they've preserved
his health to drive him before them like a lame goat
who will sacrifice himself, save them the trouble.
The merry widow's gone merely to fetch the rest
to watch vultures pick him apart, a rubble
of bone. —No, they want his business. This is a test
Ana devised. One last tease to puncture his gloom. . . .
He stepped in. The uncut kilim gleamed on the loom.

A runner—twice his height, he guessed: most wound around
the loom's bottom log. Then he saw cut yarns dangling
to one side. She had taken its twin. A light wind
swelled the tent roof. The loom creaked. An intense tingling
in his scalp as his dream of creation began
rewinding for his eyes: blue streams becoming grass,
willows transforming into the hands of a crone
outlined by a delta-mountain. "She did not miss
a single detail," Ahmet says. With the razor
he cut the top free, unspooled the rest of that night
in Antalya: snows of wool changing to summer
clouds, the weavers' black tents luminous with moonlight.
"I'm there, too—a face in the yarn-basket," he smiles.
"And Ana. She was the girl in the chamomiles."

He unlocks the third safe, withdraws a cylinder
of wool, narrow, twined with silk scarves. "I take it out
at odd times. For my sake. A kind of refresher
when business grows stale. It puts an end to doubt.
Not that the women's co-op would cooperate
in my quitting. Their rugs keep coming like blackmail.
And they sell. But I made them keep her tent." A slight
hesitation over the twine. "It's not for sale
and not," he decides, "for show. Sorry. It must stay
hers and mine." He has sent out discreet inquiries
about its unmatched twin, canvassed auctions. "I would pay
far too much to have it. Even more, if I could seize
that dream back, undream it. Ana could have kept this—
but chose the end of the world. Like the Nemesis."

 9

Any number of worlds are ending each minute—
cancer wards, highway head-ons. Still-birth. Razor flash.
Ana's world, too, he believes, ended. In Izmit,
August 1999, in the cymbal-crash
of the Anatolian Fault. Seventeen thousand
crushed in bed—dreaming, maybe, how their lives still might
surprise them—sleepers with secret worlds close at hand:
wives, husbands, children; the dead, visiting their night
with mystery-gestures, vague warnings; creation
itself, the primeval fabric rich in image
and pattern, knotted by each breath in the nation
of sleep. Seventeen thousand dreams, each dreamer a page
in the book of lost kilims. He believes Leila
foresaw where those underworlds would swallow Ana.

And half of him must keep believing her alive,
the horizons encompassing his own life's calm
epicenter: these white walls where women survive
namelessness, dispossession, and death in kilims
that collect the heavens housed in mothers, daughters,
handed down, lifeworks of prayer perfected in
the secret world designed to outlive all the slaughter
of earthquake, rape, war, the grind of centuries. Then
he steps into the back room. "Come," he says. "One last
kilim." The one Ana left him to discover
on his return from the mountains, her simplest
weave of welcome and farewell. It's his bed-cover.
Its blue border, both sky and Circassian eyes.
Its red core, her silhouette: an embrace his size.

An Indefinite Sentence of Exile in Florence, Massachusetts

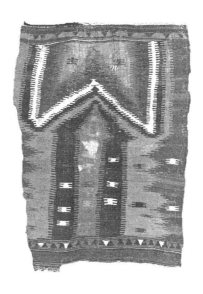

At the butcher's block in Everybody's Market,
behind the meat saw, Dom laughs at Cosmo's
old hard-on joke while stuffing kielbasa
I'm buying for backyard barbecue to show
the vegetarian neighbors my family's not deserting
serious meat, no matter what they hiss
in bean-and-tofu-tainted gossip—
so loading the frayed Nigerian jute sack
(Peace Corps, 1976) with salsa verde,
malt vinegar, garlic matzoh and sausage,
I fetch Magnolia, our hundred-pound Samoyed,
whose ancestors include White Fang and other
Jack London-style dogs, and who will eat
BBQ kielbasa but prefers vegetarian cats,
and am hailed by our postman Mr. Ronald Ragan
(Ron to friends) outside the PO to defend
a position I took in my new commercial poem,
that if flamingos ate grass, not shrimp,
they'd be grass-green, not shrimp-pink,
causing a crisis (admittedly minor)
for manufacturers and owners of lawn flamingos,

but the poem has been rejected by *Life,
Redbook, Woman's Day*, and *Ebony*,
Ron chuckles, handing me
freshly slit SASEs as he skips into
Pizza Factory to announce that their
application for tax-exempt status has
also been rejected, though A-1 Pizza
and Attila's Pizza have been awarded
multimillion-dollar contracts by

the Department of Defense to manufacture
freeze-dried pizza to spiff up the morale
of homesick Marine paratroopers stuck
on Third World missions—and it's true
that the many ex-Marine outpatients
from the local VA relieve symptoms
of post-trauma stress at A-1 or Attila's,
never at Pizza Factory, though one vet
calling himself Nebuchadnezzar
seems to eat nothing but grass he plucks
from cracks in the village fountain,
which once spouted water from the Mill River,

which rich Yankees wanted to rename
the Arno—having already upgraded
the village name from Pleasant Meadow
to Florence—honoring Tuscan silkworkers
who emigrated here to hatch silkworms,
labor communes, and revolutions,
and to fornicate with married Yankee women
on the pretext of supplying them with camisoles
and silk teddies, while the rich doctor—
and lawyer—husbands sipped from
the fountain, humming Down by the old,
not the new but the old, mill stream,
thinking Yankee money plus Italian labor
equals more Yankee money, only to see
their kids end up squandering inheritances
on pizza slices, pizza-counter girls, and, finally,
pizza franchises (*Ciao* Yale medicine,
arrivederci Harvard law)—so the Yankee
elders tried to forbid private use of silk,
public consumption of pizza, mentioning
the Arno, saying *Ciao!* to the postman,

but when they voted to strike the name
Florence, they were barred from
the Miss Florence Diner (specializing in
veal parmigian and New England boiled dinner)
with a jukebox in every booth,
and every jukebox stuffed with concertina,
mandolins, Sinatra and Como! so they
(the Yankee elders) had to confine
their persecution to Sacco & Vanzetti,
whose photos hang cold and perpetually
fresh in Miss Flo's pie safe, though Miss Flo
likes to keep everything cold—especially
the coffee, and me drinking it with windows
open to a late April snow—because
Miss Flo knows cold customers drinking
cold coffee need to buy hot veal and boiled
cabbage to regain strength and wit
enough to skip the bill, and slip
on a still-icy street, and be just barely
missed by the Volunteer Pumper Truck
on its way to douse Nebuchadnezzar

setting his matted beard afire to protest
how the endless New England winter
interferes with convalescence from
the bone-shaking nightmares brought on
by a year of jungle fighting—but Magnolia
my snow-dog has already knocked him
down to lick out his would-be Buddhist
self-immolation, and though dazed
he allows me by way of apology
to escort him to Sandy's Vietnamese Cuisine
for lemon-grass tea and lichee-nut pizza,
which Sandy (a silk-sheathed tigress) serves,

lamenting in French the pizza franchises
she left behind in Hue and Saigon—
but my errands take me back to Florence Center
to Bird's Store Since 1867
Your One and Only Stop for Indonesian
clove cigarettes (me), Italian silk
underthings (my wife), and Vermont
maple syrup (two kids), plus a stop
at Computer Farm to check their progress

on my idea for software that generates
terrific commercial poems to break open
a monster poetry market in *Cosmopolitan*
and *TV Guide* and get my face into
supermarkets, and out of these tweedy
academic quarterlies that bury my poems
on the shelves of college-library basements,
but it appears the local programmers have
applied my concepts to the random generation
of freeze-dried pizza recipes because,
as one jests, What's one flabby poet
next to a DOD contract? so I leave,
saddened that Marines will keep on
parachuting all over the world,
bellies full of computerized pizza,
instead of deserting to write poetry
and drink lemon-grass tea with me
in the pleasant meadows of Florence,
with its three dozen graveyards
and its library full of Puritan hymnals
and its one-room museum with screeching
door and screeching floor and one
passenger pigeon stuffed under

a bell jar, not to mention the tricentennial
witch-hunt festival, and crowds waving torches
outside Miss Flo's when she threatens
to throw Sinatra out of all her booth-sized
jukeboxes in favor of the Dead Kennedys
—yes, the Florentine air I breathe is rich
with the burnt-earth odor of exile
that made Ovid weep by the Black Sea
and Mandelstam cough in Vladivostok,
and that makes the vet outpatients sneeze
in memory of body hair seared by friendly
napalm strikes or attempted self-immolation,
a measure that would solve nothing for me,
since my exile includes children who
need me to fix boiled dinner, pour syrup,
apply Band-Aids and teach them something
besides the notion that Adam invented
alphabet soup and kielbasa, while Eve
invented multiplication, teacup etiquette,
and needlepoint, and that black men
make good athletes while white men make

good presidents, and women of whatever
color make good wet-nurses, as I've gathered
from their social studies primer
that my wife wants to burn though as a Jewish
Marxist-feminist she'd get tied to a Maypole,
doused with gas and lit while PTA
members prance around it, chanting passages
from Hawthorne and Jonathan Edwards,
which reminds me to save some BBQ
kielbasa to take down to the cellar
(last used by the Underground Railroad)
where my better half has been in hiding

since that riot at the VFW Friday Night Beano,
when she stood to demand that they send
a ton or two of their used kidney-bean
game pieces to Vietnam, Nicaragua,
or at least Grenada, and got us both
pelted with dry beans and chased home
through one of the newer graveyards
by a bunch of one-legged,
one-armed, one-eyed drunks—

nevertheless, I cherish her red-diaper-baby
ferocity that drove her to move us
from the gossipy dogwood haze
of Chapel Hill, where our socialist-surrealist
fervor had rooted and spread like kudzu,
although North Carolina no longer
required two arthritic hippies in its
political-poetic avant-garde, leading
my wife to declare, In Massachusetts,
we can end the witch-burning tricentennials,
the indiscriminate use of villanelles,
and the conspiracy to make the Third World
safe for freeze-dried pizza, while our kids
can learn to drink syrup straight
from the maple, and we can commute
to work and political rallies
on cross-country skis! and now she's
shivering and dirty in the cellar,
with only mice and spiders and the frowning
ghost of Harriet Tubman for company,
so I stop by Moriarty's Drugs to get her
a quart of Dr. Bronner's Peppermint Soap,

which brings All-One-God-Faith and Moral-ABC
to anyone who can read while shampooing
by candlelight on a dirt-packed cellar floor
—yet what other soapmaker writes poetry
and prints it in impossibly tiny characters
on every bottle of soap he ships out,
this blind Essene rabbi, master chemist,
whose cousins were rendered into Nazi soap?

FACE THE WORLD WITH A SMILE,

LIFE IS ALWAYS WORTHWHILE!

WE LIVE GOD'S LAW TODAY!

WE WIN FREE SPEECH OK!

I chant Dr. Bronner's bubbly praise
for the 96 billion fruit trees that will sway
in the ruins of Beirut and Tripoli,
for Abraham-Isaac-Moses-Buddha-Hillel-
Jesus-Spinoza, and add my own ad-libbed
praise for Marines who forsake
grenade launchers to read O'Hara,
drink lemon-grass tea, and bathe
multi-cultural babies in mint soap—
but seeing his other customers flee

the aisles when I chant *ALL-ONE OR NONE,*
the badly rhymed label of the entire bottle,
at the top of my voice, Moriarty (sly
American druggist) starts playing his
78 record of Harry Truman's Happy Birthday
Variations for Piano & A-Bomb
—so this vision, like most visions of peace
I have, collapses under the boogie-woogie
weight of Truman's left hand and the soundtrack

of bombs that bracketed the day of my birth
in the early fifties, when Moriarty claims
to have held a block party for McCarthy,
distributing 8×10 glossies signed
God Bless—Joe, plus plans for a backyard
bomb shelter of Moriarty's design
and barbiturate samples, in case the canned
soup ran out before the bombs did,
but Moriarty's the village liar
and the only way to discourage him
is to buy nothing he sells, so I put back
the soap, and steal some ipecac to help me

throw up the kielbasa casing later
and head home to Corticelli Street,
named for the silk-mill foreman,
a well-known socialist and little-known
surrealist, who forged a batch of letters
from Rimbaud to Dante, erotic letters,
which he preferred to read aloud under
the skirt or between the breasts of whatever
rich anemic Yankee wife he was taking
advantage of that afternoon, before strolling
home to piss away his soul into the narrow,
sluggish Mill River that tried (and failed)
to be transformed into the wine-dark
Arno, and it's in Corticelli's honor
that I step through the ruins of poison ivy
and stinging nettle to the river bank,
to translate my own homelessness
into a prismatic arc of piss, a short, brief
rainbow that is my covenant with Ovid,
Dante, Rimbaud, and Mandelstam,
who stood drunk with lethal exile
and longing at the edge of that last river,

into which all rivers and seas empty themselves,
as I try to empty myself of myself,
and fail, and stand, ruefully, shaking my dick
and my head, whistling up into a white pine
where four crows have alighted and hop
from branch to branch, full of the rust
of crow-mockery—Hey look, it's Ovid, Dante, Rimbaud,
Mandelstam, Hello, glad to see you again!
I call, inviting them to my kielbasa cookout,
since I know only the burnt odor
of serious meat and a beakful of red wine
will allow them to croak out their human memories—
but are those crow-tears I see? spurts
of pure black bile, making a quietus
of their laughter as they gaze past me,
and at what? —my children! my blond,
sugar-lipped angels, curled together
in their hammock that is stretched
in the paradise shade between two towering
sugar maples, of course, what else
can strike tears from the great flying dead
but an intimate glimpse of this simple

mortal heaven their bargain with immortality
forbade?—Hey, kids! I cry in a surprising
access of tears, sending my fingers through
their hair to wake them to this visitation
of crow-poets—then, wiping my eyes, I commence
the introductions with *My great and eternally
childless mentors, this is Seth, this is Sarah,
these two are heaven's reasons why
I remain happy as a minor asterisk
of a poet, why my heart has not collapsed
into a white-dwarf cinder beneath your fixed*

and unattainable lights—then Sarah says,
Hey, blackbirds! and Seth extends
a sleeved boy-angel wrist as a perch,
and, wisely, I think, while my feet are
underfoot, so to speak, and not in my mouth,
I go set up the barbecue and drinks—
so while the children stroke his mournful
plumage, Mandelstam begins reciting
in trochaic tetrameter the ingredients
of Siberian gruel: toenails of wolves,
whiskers of cockroaches, dissolved in a broth

of Stalin's tears, how the train to Vladivostok
rattled loose the one black tooth
in his mouth, how he composed his last poem
on a garbage heap, with a bit of barbed wire,
on a scroll of his own skin the size
of a postage stamp, one rhyming couplet
begging the labor-camp warden for a pair
of used swallow wings (I lay meat out
on shining grass, the crow-poets harry it;
the sun, almost gone, fires the crowns
of our maples to green torches; Ovid sips
Pinot Noir from the saucer of Seth's cupped palms)
—then Rimbaud scratches his head
with one claw and describes the army ants
which feasted on his mules, overloaded with rifles
and dying en route to the King of Ethiopia,
how he coaxed the ants to haul the rifles
by promising to show them Paris,
then betrayed them to the King's anteaters,
for which crime he lost his love of poetry
and ended up a poor bitter shopkeeper

on an island in the Indian Ocean, contracting
gangrene from an ant bite and dying
before he got to see Paris again
(stars salt the rain-barrel, Mandelstam,
isn't that right, on your revolutionary earth
moving closer to truth and to dread,
above the lemon-colored Neva at night—
or are the stars, as Rimbaud believes,
lice infesting the heads of fallen boy-geniuses,
white bites of hell that crack under
a mother's murderous nails?)
—then Ovid, waving his wings, shouts,
No more poetry, who wants magic?
and the kids shout, Us! so he changes Sarah
into a laurel tree and Seth into a swan,
and, as soon as I protest, I find myself mooing,
drooling hungrily at the dewy, starlit lawn
I forgot to mow yesterday, but when I bend
my bull-heavy head down for a bite,
Dante says, Ovid, that's enough, and *Poof!*
the children become sleepy children

again in my arms (they're my heroes,
Ovid, and I'm theirs, with no wish to be
morphed out of our lamp-lit constellation
of rooms among the maples, no compulsion
to hype our love's claims to a size
that strains to move the sun and all the stars,
as Dante drove himself to do, and so
broke his voice), and suddenly it's late,
and Dante, perched on my lawn-chair,
takes umbrage at my thought, clacks
his hooked beak and caws something sharp,
like *Curfew!* or *Ecce Homo!*

and the crow-poets fly after him, back into
their star-charted exile, leaving four feathers,
which are tickets, I guess, good for
a one-way family trip to the underworld,
so sticking the feathers behind my ear
I head to the cellar door, kicking it lightly
three times (all-clear signal to wife),
and look up at the stars (goodnight,
good-bye, who knows which?) before carrying

the heavy sweetness of children underground.

NOTES

THE BOOK OF JOEL
Dedicated to Joel Rossi, September 12, 1980—August 16, 1999: nineteen sonnets for nineteen years.

33: "I'm going to be perfect, starting now" alludes to the Built to Spill song "Randy Described Eternity."

34: "The Dyer's Head" puns on Auden's *The Dyer's Hand*.

35: A white Les Paul hangs by the cash till: like me, Joel played electric guitar. This is his Epiphone Les Paul.

38: "*Nuites Americains*" is more about the "day for night" process of shooting night scenes at day than Truffaut's film.

40: "*Tikkun*": *tikkun olam*, Hebrew for "repairing the world."

THE KILIM DREAMING

52: "This land like the head of a mare galloping from Asia / to quench its thirst in the Mediterranean": Nazim Hikmet.

53: *Abrash*: subtle changes within single-color areas on kilims, often due to dye pots being so stuffed with yarn that the dye does not penetrate evenly. *Mihrab*: a niche in the wall of a mosque that indicates the direction of the Kaaba in Mecca. Mihrabs on prayer rugs are positioned to point toward Mecca. Multiple mihrabs indicate a family prayer rug.

55: *Salvar*: baggy trousers, traditionally worn with *entari*, a long robe.

56: Circassian: indigenous tribal people of the NW Caucasus, also known as Adyghe and Cherkess. In 1864, Russian imperialists forced a mass migration of nine-tenths of the Circassian population; many went to Anatolia.

78: "Lot four: this composition of six arches" is based on the kilim featured on the cover of Cathryn Cootner's *Anatolian Kilims*. The kilims about which Cootner writes are in San Franciso's DeYoung Museum.

The Goddess From Anatolia (1989) by James Mellaart is controversial—many regard his claims and images as an elaborate hoax. But it influenced the rug trade for some time. The Neolithic site Çatal Hüyük continues to be excavated.

ACKNOWLEDGMENTS

Grateful acknowledgment is made to the following publications in which these poems first appeared.

Portions of "The Book of Joel" appeared in the *Marlboro Review* and *Water~Stone Review*.

"An Indefinite Sentence of Exile in Florence, Massachusetts" first appeared in *ZYZZYVA*.

About the Author

Robert Hill Long is the award-winning author of three previous books of poetry: *The Power to Die*, *The Work of the Bow*, and *Effigies*. He has been published widely in such journals as *Poetry*, *New Letters*, *Puerto del Sol*, and *The Best American Poetry* series. He lives in Eugene, Oregon.